Kenyan Organic Intellectuals
Reflect on the Legacy of
Pio Gama Pinto

Edited by
Lewis Maghanga,
Nicholas Mwangi

Daraja Press

Published by
Daraja Press
https://darajapress.com

ISBN: 9781990263279

Cover design: Kate McDonnell

Library and Archives Canada Cataloguing in Publication

Title: Kenyan organic intellectuals reflections on the legacy of Pio Gama
    Pinto / edited by Nicholas Mwangi & Lewis Maghanga.
Names: Mwangi, Nicholas, editor. | Maghanga, Lewis, editor.
Identifiers: Canadiana 20210327790 | ISBN 9781990263279 (softcover)
Subjects: LCSH: Pinto, Pio Gama, 1927-1965—Influence. | LCSH:
    Social justice—Kenya
Classification: LCC HM671 .K46 2021 | DDC 303.3/72096762—dc23

CONTENTS

FOREWORD BY LINDA GAMA-PINTO

I am honored to have been asked to contribute a few words about my father, Pio Gama-Pinto (Pio Pinto) to preface a new book of reflections on his work and legacy. The contributors to this volume are renowned thinkers and activists on the rights of oppressed peoples in Kenya and thus everywhere. Pio would have been surprised and humbled that such a group would 'spill so much ink' writing about him.

The evening of my father's assassination I remember a huge bonfire in the front yard by the room he used as his office. I could make out figures, the heat from the flames making their silhouettes waver as they fed papers into the fire. 'What did they burn?' I asked my mother later. 'All your father's writings my dear.' 'But why?' 'Because they were afraid.' 'Was Papa afraid?' 'Yes,' she replied, 'but some things are more important than fear.'

His writings were lost. So, what remains of Pio are the stories of his actions and the actions themselves. And as the contributors here attest – there is a wonderful consistency in his actions that allows us to reconstruct his philosophy and his values, despite the destruction of his written work. This legacy of brave, selfless work for the improvement of the oppressed was deliberate, purposeful, tactical, and grounded in values of justice and equality. He sought no glory, no position. It was only on the urging of my mother, his wife Emma, that he put his name forward for the Special Selected Member of Parliament. In 1963 he was elected a Member of the Central Legislative Assembly and in July 1964 was appointed a Specially Elected Member of the House of Representatives.

He was as surprised as anyone that he won.

He used that position as a gadfly – stinging the powerful, not allowing them to get away with their corrupt dealings! That sealed his fate. I believe however, that had he lived, he would have continued buzzing and biting. He could not stand the hypocrisy of the new 'elite', knowing what the Forest Fighters, the men, and the women, sacrificed for an independent Kenya.

In October 2021, Emma Gama-Pinto, Pio beloved wife passed away. Not to subtract from Pio's achievements, but a special note must be made of Emma, who never asked him to stop, never asked him to 'choose'. She was as much a part of the 'struggle' in keeping Pio strong and focussed on his goal of freeing people from all forms of poverty: of mind, spirit and body.

We need heroes to inspire us when we tire. Pio and Emma are my heroes.

Pio with integrity and humility, sacrificed all for country. Emma lived with such ferocity that she inspired many to aim beyond their self-perceived limits and achieve greatness.

I hope this book of reflections about Pio will inspire you to live your values with humility and ferocity!

Linda Gama-Pinto
Ottawa, August 30, 2021

INTRODUCTION BY SHIRAZ DURRANI

Pio Gama Pinto was born on March 31, 1927.
He was under British detention & restriction from 1954-1959.
He was assassinated on February 24, 1965.

That, in brief, is the story of Pio Gama Pinto. Since his assassination, there is just one brief appearance of his name — in 1966. This was in a booklet edited by Ambu Patel: *Pio Gama Pinto, Independent Kenya's First Martyr: Socialist and Freedom Fighter*. Then total silence. No meaningful mention of Pinto in newspapers, radio, TV, books, history, research. His enemies, who had him assassinated, feared the mention of his name even after his death. They feared most his vision and commitment to equality, justice and socialism. The British Colonial Government destroyed or hid all papers related to Pinto. Similarly, the KANU Governments of Jomo Kenyatta, Daniel arap Moi and all the succeeding governments to date fear him in death as much as the British and the first KANU government feared him in life. They have imposed a 'silence' about him with ruthlessness and violence that showed their fear of this one man. They refused to release secret files held by the government, even to the Truth, Justice and Reconciliation Commission which tried to probe his assassination in 2013.

That silence would have removed Pinto's name from the history of Kenya for ever — but for a fact which the British and Kenya Governments had not reckoned with: History never dies; oppression and exploitation always give rise to resistance, especially among the young; those who lost their loved ones, land and property can never forget the atrocities of the invading horde of White settlers from South Africa and Britain who the British Government supported and then went on to 'legalise' their loot by imposing a comprador regime at independence. With the blessings of the imperialists, the new regime carried on similar looting and atrocities.

The Moi regime ruled with guns, massacres, murders, jailing and disappearance of thousands. It took advantage of the 1982 Coup to start a more ruthless oppression. In spite of, as well as because of, that resistance also intensified. The Kenyan youth, many born after independence, started their search for the real history of Kenya. They wanted to know more about their history. The student organisation (SONU) at the University of Nairobi published articles in the *University Platform* on Mau Mau, Kimathi, Makhan

Singh and Pio Gama Pinto. That was the first public mention of Pinto since 1966. This was followed by articles on Pinto in *The Standard* in September 1984. The silent embargo on Pinto and his vision was broken. But the Establishment ensured that this was covered up and Pinto and his history were suppressed once more.

Yet Pinto was never forgotten among the progressive left which had remained active all through the period of repression by the various KANU governments. They celebrated his achievement not only in private, but in public too, whenever conditions allowed. For example, the event, *Commemoration of the 50th Anniversary of the Assassination of Shujaa Pio Gama Pinto* held at the Mazingira Institute in Nairobi on 7 March 2015. Vidija (2015) reported on it:

On Saturday afternoon the Mazingira Institute in Nairobi hosted a special commemoration of the 50th anniversary of his assassination.

The guest of honour at the event was Chief Justice Willy Mutunga. He described Pinto as a freedom fighter, detainee, socialist, political strategist, a focused journalist and family-man who loved and cherished everything around him. Among those who participated in the event were Gitu wa Kahengeri, Yash Pal Ghai, Pheroze Nowrojee, Rev Timothy Njoya, Muthoni Likimani and Dr Elizabeth Orchidson-Mazrui and Firoze Manji. One of the presentations at the event (Manji, 2018) was reproduced in Durrani (2018). Pheroze Nowrojee went on to publish an important (and perhaps the only) book on Pinto since 1966, *Pio Gama Pinto: Patriot for social Justice* (Nowrojee, 2007) which gave many hidden facts about Pinto and remains an important resource on Pinto to-date.

Thus when the book, *Pio Gama Pinto, Kenya's Unsung Martyr 1927-1965* (Durrani, 2018) came out in 2018 with a public launch in Nairobi, it brought together all those who had been keeping the memory of Pinto alive. In a matter of a few years, there have been several developments that have forced the story of Pio Gama Pinto back to centre stage in Kenya: forcing the issue of stolen lands back on national agenda; forcing issues of equality and justice for working people as *the* agenda for Kenya today.

The following are just a few initiatives on Pio Gama Pinto:

1. A group has been formed to look after Pinto's neglected grave at the City Park. It has also commissioned a bust of Pinto to be installed at the cemetery.
2. Young people from Mathare Social Justice Centre (MSJC) visit Pinto grave and learn his history following their study on Pinto at Mathare.

3. Various readings and activities on Pinto take place at Ukombozi Library.
4. Social Justice Centres take up Pinto studies.
5. Until Everyone is Free: A seven-part podcast on Pinto in Sheng' is making the rounds among people in Kenya and overseas.
6. The social media has seen numerous postings on Pinto, his life and his assassination.

The latest on the scene is this book, *Kenya Organic Intellectuals Reflect on the Legacy of Pio Gama Pinto* (edited by Nicholas Mwangi and Lewis Maghanga Njuguna) from activists at the Social Justice Centres and the Ukombozi Library, carrying on the tradition of Kenyan youth to explore and understand history as a guide to action. History never dies — 'A thousand beacons from the spark he bore' have started rising. Nothing can extinguish this new fire in Kenya. The history of resistance cannot be suppressed for ever. There comes a time when the hidden chapters of history and the crimes of the ruling class are exposed. That time has come for Pio Gama Pinto. It is the brave ones, armed with a clear understanding of history, undaunted by batons and bullets of the ruling class, who are taking people's history back to people. Liberating minds. Preparing for new battles. That time is here. The very act by the writers in this book to read and reflect on Pio Gama Pinto indicates that clearly.

What has inspired these writers to take up the study of a man assassinated over half a century ago, when most of them were not even born? They represent a generation growing up under capitalism. They are the ones who have seen and suffered the consequence of inequality and injustice that capitalism has brought to Kenya. And they represent the generation that says *Tunakataa!* They refuse to accept the poverty, the looting, the massacres and the daily police harassment and killings that the state uses to suppress working people. Reading and reflecting on Pio Gama Pinto is an appropriate way to say 'No' to the capitalist *status quo*. Pinto was, after all, the one who said 'No' to capitalist injustices at the very beginning of independence.

The struggle for socialism is long and painful, requiring many sacrifices. However, without such struggles, this generation and future generations will be condemned to poverty and injustice. By taking up the study of Pinto, the writers of this book have made a commitment to struggle for socialism, equality and justice for working people. They are looking back into history to organise a better future for all. They are not just a few individuals taking up the struggle. They are part of a larger community, organised and acting for change as shown by the section, *About the Contributors*, at the end of the book. Each contributor is an activist among various communities. It is this that gives a greater significance to their reflections and to this book. These are not the reflections of only 14 individuals. These are reflections and aspirations of their communities, of millions of working people in Kenya whose voice these 14 represent.

These voices would not have reached everyone in Kenya, in Africa, indeed all working people around the world, had their reflections not been committed to print. Daraja Press needs to be congratulated for publishing these Reflections. Their support also indicates that the voice of working people of Kenya is not calling out in isolation. It indicates that they have supporters thousands of miles from Kenya, in Canada, as in many other countries. And that their struggle is also the struggle of all working people who have had capitalism imposed on them by imperialism. The struggle for socialism in Kenya is part of the struggle in Africa and the world against exploitation and oppression. These Reflections by 14 courageous Kenyans are a challenge to the entire population of Kenya to reflect on where we have been and to work towards achieving the vision that Pio Gama Pinto had — 'a democratic, African, socialist state in which the people have the right to be free from economic exploitation and the right to social equality'. It is the vision of working people in Kenya and the world. The struggle continues.

The Struggle for Pinto's History

The story of Pinto is not only his story — it is the story of Mau Mau, it is the story of those who fought in forests and towns, it is the story of all those who have suffered and are still suffering the ravages of capitalism in Kenya. While there is a revived interest in Pinto, his life, his vision and his activities, there remains a large gap in his history that prevents a full record of his achievements to be written. His story remains incomplete and untold with the loss of his own papers and the refusal of the British and Kenyan governments to release documents on him. The refusal by the Kenya government to initiate or even support research on the history of Mau Mau and Kenya's war of independence has also meant that oral and other records from those who knew Pinto has been allowed to die over time. Particularly relevant is the lack of information on Pinto as a member and activist of Mau Mau. The evidence mentioned in Durrani (2018) points to Pinto being an active member of Mau Mau. The book also mentions an interview with Mzee Wachaga wa Muthami (a Mau Mau veteran) in Nairobi on August 5, 2013 where he confirms that Pinto was a member of Mau Mau. That he has not been seen as part of Mau Mau has robbed the movement as well as Pinto of an important aspect of their history. It is not only Pinto who has been robbed of his history, but also people like Mzee Wachaga wa Muthami and thousands of the Mau Mau activists and supporters. Pinto and his life cannot be fully appreciated until the real history of all these people and of Mau Mau is researched, documented and made available. The sad irony is that many of these veterans are dying in poverty, as did Mzee Wachaga wa Muthami whose life and death reinforce the need to restore Kenya's history — and achieve Pinto vision of a society where 'people have the right to be free from economic exploitation and the right to social equality'. Mzee Wachaga wa Muthami's history reflects that of thousands of others (Durrani, Shiraz and Gathui wa Manyara, 2013):

> We were poor. Father's land taken over by the British colonial government – 10 acres (?), and he was left without a shamba.It was difficult to find money for food, school fees etc, so we sold our livestock to survive. My father was a member of KCA (Kikuyu Central Association). My grandfather was Muthami Muguma, of the Njenga rikka. [1]

Gathui wa Manyara provides further information on Mzee Wacaga wa Muthami:

> In his later days, Mzee Wacaga was a peasant farmer in Molo and actively involved in the second liberation. He moved to his mother's house in one of the colonial villages near Wangige on the outskirts of Nairobi – commonly known as "Cuba"—after the death of his wife and only daughter. When the Kibaki Government came to power it officially recognised Mau Mau as a Freedom Fighter Movement, rather than a terrorist organisation. As a result, many Mau Mau combatants began to hope that this government would bring about the change they had been longing for. Wacaga with a few others requested the government for funds to build Mau Mau Resource Centres across the country, but were not successful.

On 25th July 2017, Mzee Wacaga fell outside his house, and was unable to walk. He was taken to hospital where surgery was recommended. Unable to

---

1. Notes from an interview of Mzee Wacaga wa Muthami (a Mau Mau veteran) in Nairobi on August 5, 2013. Interviewees: Shiraz Durrani and Gathui wa Manyara. Manyara provided additional information on Mzee Wacaga later in private correspondence with the author..

raise the required funds, relatives took him back home where he passed away on 1st September 2017, at the age of 86.

It is conditions such as this which allow veterans of the war of independence to die in poverty that Pio Gama Pinto fought against and gave his life to change. The tragedy is not only for Pinto, but for all the Mau Mau combatants and activists, for all working people of Kenya. Capitalism and imperialism have captured the country, its people and its resources for their own private profit. The struggle for liberation *has* to continue.

References

Shiraz Durrani and Gathui wa Manyara (2013): Quoted from Notes from an interview of Mzee Wacaga wa Muthami (a Mau Mau veteran) in Nairobi on August 5, 2013. Unpublished. Manyara provided additional information on Mzee Wacaga later in private correspondence with the author.

Durrani, Shiraz (ed) (2018): *Pio Gama Pinto, Kenya's Unsung Martyr 1927-1965*. Nairobi: Vita Books.

Manji, Firoze: Tribute to Pio Gama Pinto: Memorials are more about the future than about the past. In Durrani, Shiraz (2018) pp. 162-166.

Mwangi Nicholas and Lewis Maghanga Njuguna (eds.) (2021): *Kenya Organic Intellectuals' Reflect on the Legacy of Pio Gama Pinto*. Daraja Press: Quebec.

Nowrojee, Pheroze (2007): Pio Gama Pinto: Patriot for Socialist Justice. Nairobi: Sasa Sema.

Patel, Ambu (Ed., 1966) : Pio Gama Pinto, Independent Kenya's First Martyr: Socialist and Freedom Fighter. Nairobi: Pan African Press.

Vidija, Patrick (2015): Kenyans remember freedom fighter Pio Gama Pinto. *The Star*. 11-03-2015. Available at: https://www.the-star.co.ke/sasa/society/2015-03-11-kenyans-remember-freedom-fighter-pio-gama-pinto/ [Accessed: 04-10-2021].

Shiraz Durrani
October 4, 2021

NOTES ON PIO GAMA PINTO

Pio Gama Pinto (31 March 192 to 24 February 1965)[1] was a Kenyan journalist, politician and freedom fighter. He was a socialist leader who dedicated his life to the liberation of the Kenyan people and became independent Kenya's first martyr in 1965. He was born in Nairobi to a family of Konkani Goan Catholic descent. He studied science at Karnatak College, Dharwar, India, for two years before joining the Indian Air Force in 1944 as an apprentice ground engineer. He then took up a job in the Posts and Telegraph office in Bombay, participated in a general strike and became a founding member of the Goa National Congress whose aim was the liberation of Goa from Portuguese rule. His political activism soon made it necessary for him to return to Kenya in 1949 to avoid being arrested and deported to the Tarrafal concentration camp in Cape Verde.

After a succession of clerical jobs, he became involved in local politics aimed at overthrowing British colonial rule in Kenya. He turned to journalism and worked with the *Colonial Times* and the *Daily Chronicle*. In 1954, five months after his marriage to Emma Dias, he was rounded up in the notorious Operation Anvil and spent the next four years in detention on Manda Island. He was kept in confinement from early 1958 until October 1959 at Kabarnet. In 1960 he founded the Kenya African National Union (KANU) newspaper *Sauti Ya KANU*, and later, *Pan African Press*, of which he subsequently became Director and Secretary. Pinto played an active role in campaigning for KANU during the 1961 elections which it won. In 1963 he was elected a Member of the Central Legislative Assembly and in July 1964 was appointed a Specially Elected Member of the House of Representatives. He worked to establish the Lumumba Institute in 1964 to train KANU party officials.

On 24 February 1965, at the age of 38, Pinto was shot and killed at close range in the driveway of his home in Nairobi. His daughter was in his car when he was shot. Pinto was the first Kenyan politician to be assassinated after Independence. He was survived by his wife, Emma and his three daughters Linda, Malusha and Tereshka. The assassination was clearly

---

1. Source: https://en.wikipedia.org/wiki/Pio_Gama_Pinto

politically motivated because of his political opposition to the growing neo-colonialisation of Kenya under Jomo Kenyatta's regime.

Pio Pinto's colleagues established a Pinto Trust Fund to help his widow and family to which a number of governments, including China and Tanzania, contributed. In September 1965, his widow, Emma Gama Pinto ,was invited to Santiago, Chile, to receive a posthumous prize awarded to her husband by the International Organisation of Journalists for his contribution to journalism and to the liberation of African countries from foreign domination and exploitation. In 2008, Kenya released a series of four stamps titled Heroes of Kenya, one of which depicted Pinto.

INTRODUCTION

Nicholas Mwangi and Lewis Maghanga Njuguna

History is not everything, but it is a starting point. History is a clock that people use to tell their political and cultural time of day. It is a compass they use to find themselves on the map of human geography. It tells them where they are but, more importantly, what they must be. —Pan-Africanist writer and historian, John Henrik Clarke.

This book on Pio Gama Pinto has been produced in the tradition of 'looking back, in order to move forward', to not only salvage history but also to use it as a mirror to reflect on the current political, economic and social conditions in Kenya. The essays that appear in the booklet are a product of the efforts and dedication of young women and men under the banner of the 'Organic Intellectuals Network' in Kenya. We use the concept of 'organic intellectual' as developed by Antonio Gramsci.

Members of the Organic Intellectual Network selected the book *Pio Gama Pinto: Kenya's Unsung Martyr* 1927-1965 edited by Shiraz Durrani (Vita Books, 2018)[1] as a basis for discussion for celebrating and remembering the life of Pio Gama Pinto, Kenya first martyr, a dedicated and selfless individual involved in the struggle for freedom in Kenya. Pinto has not been fully appreciated and recognized for his efforts in the fight for independence and post-independence struggles that were characterized by ideological confrontation between capitalism and socialism. Each of the 14 participants in the discussions were asked to write their reflections on what they had learned, based on their daily struggles as activists, students and revolutionary community organizers in their communities. These discussions were accompanied by several activities at the beginning of 2021 aimed at remembering Pio Gama Pinto on the 56th anniversary of his assassination. These activities included reflections at his memorial grave and the production of a podcast.

---

1. This anthology comprised contributions from Emma Gama Pinto, Pheroze Nowrojee, Shiraz Durrani, Willy Mutunga, Angelo Faria, Rosario Da Gama Pinto, Firoze Manji, materials on Pinto compiled by Awaaz Magazine, Kamoji Wachira, Dinesh Singh, Malcom MacDonald, Fenner Brockway, Makhan Singh, Joseph Murumbi, selections from Pinto's own writings, photographs and other documentations.

This book aims at retrieving and providing a genuine national direction for the struggles of Kenyans based on historical clarity devoid of any obscurity and distortion. It is our hope that these simplified reflections will introduce Pio Gama Pinto and socialism to the Kenyan people and across the world.

PIO GAMA PINTO

Kenya's Unsung Martyr
1927-1965

Edited by
Shiraz Durrani

REFLECTION 1: ESTHER WAIGUMO NJOKI

Until April 9, 2021, I knew very little about Pio Gama Pinto. Well, actually what I knew was that he was one of the many assassinated politicians in Kenya. However, on this day something happened that would later trigger my interest towards knowing more about his work and his ideology. It eventually made me read the book *Pio Gama Pinto: Kenya's Unsung Martyr*.

A comrade friend had suggested that we take a reflection walk. So, on that day in April, we walked all the way from the informal settlements of Mathare to Muthaiga and then proceeded to City Park. Soon, I would see a cemetery and I must admit at first, I freaked out. After taking a few more steps, there I was standing beside Pio Gama's grave. My comrade friend knew a lot about Pio Pinto and I stood in awe as he narrated how Pio came out of prison after detention without shoes as he had given them away. I learned how he came to be assassinated and had been buried in the same grave as his father. I learned how his best friend Joseph Murumbi came to be buried just a few meters from him, now known as the Murumbi Memorial. By the end of that reflection, I settled on reading more about Pio Pinto.

Emma Gama Pinto, his wife, feels that despite having many people who referred to Pio as a communist and a socialist, the best word that fits his description is as a humanist. He was simply a man of the people and he upheld humanity in his time. It is even more interesting when his wife admits that she never knew how much money Pio Gama earned, because he gave much of it away to support the widows of the freedom fighters. This is simple humanity at its best and we should all learn from these acts and embark on saving humanity since currently, I feel, it has been jeopardized and so many people are willing to exchange humanity for their own selfish gain, including the current increase in cases of extra-judicial executions and other evils. By all cost, we must save humanity!

Pio Gama Pinto is a symbol of resistance to all evils affecting the people. During his time, he courageously resisted and exposed colonialism, imperialism and capitalism which were the evils that the working people of Kenya needed to defeat. Today, 56 years since his assassination, Kenya is still facing the same evils of imperialism, capitalism and we now have neocolonialism. These evils have resulted to high levels of poverty and so many people cannot even afford basic needs. Many of us are living in shanties with very poor conditions and having food to put on the table is not even guaranteed.

Pio Pinto was a political detainee for five years 1954 to 1959, commencing shortly after his marriage to Emma. While in detention, he used the letters his wife often sent him to teach other detainees how to read. He was determined to educate and liberate his fellow detainees. This also poses a big challenge in our current quest for social justice as there is a need for us to ensure that we educate the masses. There is power in the masses and for us to win the fight against all injustices, the masses should be well empowered so that we all speak in one voice.

Pinto was an all-rounded man and his commitment towards what he lived for is up to today unquestionable. His efforts are evident in how he was able to come through whenever needed. As the book states:

> When it was time to write political and legal cases for people's rights, Pinto was there. When it was time to develop working class and anti-imperialist ideologies, Pinto was there. When it was time to face the enemy with guns, Pinto was there. When it was time to support victims of colonial and neo colonialism terrorism, Pinto was there. When it was time to take a political stand after independence, Pinto was there. When it was time to make personal and family sacrifices for a greater cause, Pinto was there. And when the end came, when it was time to stand for his principles and to die for his country, Pinto was there.

It is so unfortunate that despite Pio's contributions towards making Kenya free from social inequality and economic exploitation, the then President Kenyatta's regime did not recognize his efforts. Many years after his assassination, Pio is still being referred to as a Kenya's unsung martyr. He is one of the people we should be celebrating. They are our heroes and our role models. It is entirely up to us to make sure that such people as well as people such as Maina wa Kinyatti are not completely forgotten. They lived for others and generations to come and the ball is in our court to ensure that we carry this same spirit until the end. Long live the undying spirit of Pio Gama Pinto!

REFLECTION 2: LENA ANYUOLO

Pio Gama Pinto was a Kenyan Goan born on March 31, 1927 in Kenya. He was a key organizer with the Kenya Land and Freedom Army, he was instrumental in the formation of a radical trade union movement in Kenya, an anti-imperialist publisher and journalist in colonial and post-colonial Kenya. As a freedom fighter, he participated in the independence movement of Goa as a founder member of the Goa National Congress that worked to free Goa from Portuguese rule. As a Pan-Africanist, he supported independence movement in Mozambique, Angola, Guinea Bissau, Comoros Island, South Africa, Guyana, Congo and Cabo Verde, and often housed freedom fighters who needed to hide from repressive colonial governments. He was assassinated on February 24, 1965, a few days after the assassination of Malcolm X on February 21, 1965. He was killed shortly after he had met with Malcolm X and they had planned to charge the US government with human rights violations at the UN.

He supported independent journalism by using his skills as a publisher and journalist to unite the working class and shed light on capitalism and imperialism as the main contradictory forces against the struggle for liberation, and not the racial and tribal divisions perpetrated by the colonial media. He aimed to bring the discussion on socialism to the mainstream as the only way in which independence from British colonial rule would benefit every patriotic Kenyan and not just a few. Using his networks as a journalist, he set up links of international solidarity with comrades in the UK, India, USA, which he used to amplify people's struggle against colonialism, and expose the atrocities of the British rule in Kenya. Moreover, he mobilized these networks for funds to set up the Lumumba Institute, a school intended for ideological training of KANU party cadres. The school was later shut down by Jomo Kenyatta in 1965, then president of Kenya i

Many factors contributed to his assassination at his home on 6, Lower Kabete Road – now the site of the Sarit Centre Mall. Pinto's plan to draft a counter document to what was *Sessional Paper No. 10,* written by Tom Mboya for Kenyatta government, and his exposure of the theft by Jomo Kenyatta of British funds sent to the Kenyan government for the purposes of resettling the landless due to the war for independence, put him in the path of the assassin's bullet. Pinto proposed a ceiling on individual land ownership of 500 acres, equitable distribution of wealth, and just rewards for Kenya

Land and Freedom Army (KFLA) fighters. Together with Oginga Odinga, he had already mobilized support of 98 of 158 Members of Parliament in support of his proposals, thus making Kenyatta and Mboya's document of unbridled capitalism (erroneously named 'African Socialism) unpopular. Had he been successful, it would have led to a repeat election where Kenyatta would potentially lose his seat as president of Kenya to Oginga Odinga.

As journalists reporting within our movements and documenting the struggles of common people, we can draw lessons from the life of Pinto. These are that we can use our privileges as writers and access to networks for the benefit of the people. It is easy to be drawn to the lavish life of media personalities who mine ethnic divisions for sensational news stories which are rewarded by imperialism. However, as socialists, it is paramount that we stick to reporting the facts and base our analysis on the class question in Kenya, which is the primary contradiction. At the same time, we must remain politically grounded through study so that our documenting does not end up being co-opted by populist narratives such as a the one currently ongoing about 'hustler vs. dynasty'. On the surface, it may seem that there is a rising class consciousness among the people of Kenya, but this is smoke and mirrors as the discourse does little to benefit the working classes. It is the ruling class co-opting radical language to settle political scores and further their selfish agenda of super-exploitation of the working class using neocolonial relationships with 'developed countries'.

Another lesson socialist archivists can learn from the life of Pinto is the importance of an independent people's media. Pinto mobilized his networks to set up a printing press together with James Gichuru, Joseph Murumbi and Oginga Odinga. The Pan-African press published three newspapers, *Sauti ya Mwafrika*, *Pan African*, and *Nyanza Times*. Prior to this, Pinto had set up and worked in independent African publications that championed the cause against imperialism and British colonial rule. Without these independently run outlets, it would have been very difficult to mobilize patriotic Kenyans towards organizing for independence. History is told from the perspective of the alleged conqueror. Therefore, as socialists working towards an equitable society, we do not expect imperialist media houses owned by the oppressing class to correctly tell our stories. That is why it is important to gather our skills towards establishing blog sites, websites, media pages, print publications that are grounded in class struggle to spread propaganda that is pro-working-class people.

During Pinto's detention at Manda Island, we get a glimpse of the deplorable colonial prison conditions. in an interview, Emma Pinto recounts how reading Shakespeare helped Pinto not to commit suicide.

Unsurprisingly, nothing has changed since independence, and the gulags that the British set up to torture suspected KLFA fighters and sympathizers still exist today. Prisoners in Kenya work in slave like conditions and the *Kenya Prisons Enterprise Corporation Order 2018,* established the Kenya Prisons Enterprise Corporation, a state corporation, with a board of directors and CEO, operating as a business entity, to increase revenue of the prisons. This had turned prison labor into slave labor subject to capitalist laws of demand and supply. Currently, the prison labor wage is between 10 cents for the lowest paid prisoner, and 20 cents for the highest paid prisoner engaged in skilled work[1]. Pinto used his media networks and privileges to amplify the deplorable conditions of forced labor and starvation at Manda Island to agitate for better treatment of inmates. Because nothing has changed fifty-eight years after independence, it is still upon us to agitate for better treatment of prisoners, most of whom are remand detainees. We need to agitate for faster hearing and sentencing , alternative methods of justice that are not punitive, and eventually, as we set up socialist and communist societies—abolition of prisons.

Finally, we can draw a lesson in conscious international solidarity from the life of Pinto. Pio Gama Pinto used his friends and comrade to mobilize funds to set up the Lumumba Institute which was meant to train KANU party cadres on anti-imperialist ideology. Despite it being shut down in 1965, we get a brief understanding on the level of political consciousness of Pinto. He understood that the fight against imperialism required a concerted effort of all working-class people, not just in Kenya alone, which is why he was able to convince comrades from different parts of the world to contribute towards the formation of this centre. As socialists, we often get caught up in the ravages of capitalism within our own countries and communities that we forget to see the bigger picture and engage others outside our spheres of influence. This can elongate our fight and dangerously isolate us, making us an easy target for imperialist and neocolonial forces. It is important to remember to unite our efforts for the working class beyond racial and national constraints.

Long live the undying spirit of Pio Gama Pinto!

---

1. https://whownskenya.com/index.php/2019/03/13/daily-salary-of-prisoners-in-kenya/. 20 Kenya cents is equivalent to USD0.002.

Application of the life of Pinto

In the social justice movement, the spirit of Pinto lives on through the emergence of groups of cadres synthesizing theory and tactics of liberation based on our experience of the freedom struggle of our time. In a class society, there are two types of intellectuals, those in service of capitalist economy, politics, and social organization, and those in service of socialist economy and political organization as the ideology of the oppressed for liberation from the exploitation of their labor by capital. I reflect on Pinto as an organic intellectual in that he was an individual within the mass base movement for independence in Kenya, Goa, and greater Afrika, who used his knowledge in service of the liberation of workers and peasants towards a communal ownership of the means of production. To do this, an individual must first be educated in revolutionary ideology of the working class. Pinto belonged to a study group called the Kenya African Study Union which was the ideological wing of the Kenya African Union. In the social justice movement, Ukombozi Library, and the Revolutionary Socialist League are spaces for self-cultivation.

It is necessary to have organic intellectuals as it negates hierarchies of knowledge extraction. Where those who have conventional markers of education such as a university degree undermine lived reality of workers. Instead, such elitist individuals will use ghettos and other organized community groups for their own interest of career advancement. This happens primarily in the form of research that hardly benefit the community. Moreover, the knowledge generated is inaccessible to the workers due to language barriers, and expensive paywalls to access academic journals where this information is published. The slums are therefore sites of extraction for universities just like the lands of Afrika are sites of extraction for precious metals and minerals for big oil companies. Not that an organization should not have advanced academics within its space. No. Rather we must have a hybrid approach to knowledge generated based on class consciousness. University students who immerse themselves among the ghetto youth provide an alternative outlook to the hopelessness of poverty and capitalist violence in the slums. In this way, ghetto youth are organized into a critical mass to effect change on their conditions instead of falling victim to drug addiction and 'horizontal violence' due to desperation. Instead, through a political instrument that is socialist, understand the reasons for their underdevelopment in contrast to the central business district – the nucleus of the metropolis. In this way, conditions of oppression are demystified from idealistic world view to a dialectical and materialistic world view towards releasing full revolutionary potential of the proletariat. At the same time, the revolutionary potential of university students is maintained through interaction with the mass base, dismantling the hierarchy of bourgeois education in the service of capitalism.

NGOs further hegemonize capitalist knowledge by engaging in labor exploitation where our labor output as social justice activists is not adequately compensated. Moreover, we hardly own our intellectual output as we do not have the rights to the researchers, reports, and data generated for NGOs. NGOs as a 'compromise' of capitalism still operate on class basis where a university graduate will be paid more than a community researcher simply for having a degree.

To counter this, within the movement, there exist spaces for independent journalism, memory and reflection in favor of a proletarian revolution. These are, *Ukombozi Review, Kenya Socialist, Hood TV, Until Everyone is Free* podcast. International platforms such as *Review of African Political Economy,* and *Africa is a Country*, kindle the emerging cell of organic intellectuals within the social justice movement. It is an effective alliance based on the common principle of social justice – which helps to amplify workers' struggle for the purpose of international solidarity. These provide room for knowledge exchange with comrades all over the world, building the spirit of Pan-Africanism while nurturing organic knowledge base of the movement. The *Travelling Theatre* of the social justice centres, as a theatre of the oppressed, decentralizes learning structure from the rigid classroom, top-down approach of banking knowledge.

To conclude my reflection, individually, it is not possible to address the issue of capitalism and imperialism. Collectively, we need to constantly sharpen ourselves through theory and practice and be part of an organized workers movement. As a writer and activist, to make sure that the work that I generate resonates with the masses towards class abolition. I believe this is no time for liberal poetry and literature that is just hopeless drama of the bourgeois and their liberal lives. Everything we do artistically as artists and activists should be in service of workers. That is the greatest continuity I can give to the revolutionary legacy of Pio Gama Pinto and the struggle for total liberation of Afrika from imperialism

REFLECTION 3: GACHEKE GACHIHI

'If I have been extinguished, yet there rise a thousand beacons from the Spark I bore '

Walking from Mathare Valley through Mau Mau Road, as you cross the foot bridge along Thika Road, that connects Mathare and City Park cemetery where Pio Gama Pinto was buried, you meet hundreds of working class people coming from middle class Parklands Estate, walking as they pass through Pio Gama Pinto Grave adjacent to the Joseph and Sheila Murumbi Mausoleum heading back to Mathare slums where Pio Gama Pinto helped set up a Mau Mau War Council City headquarters before he was taken to detention in 1954. This serves as a reminder that the struggle for social justice is still unfinished. As Comrade Firoze Manji has written in *Pio Gama Pinto: Kenyans Unsung Martyrs:* there is a similarity between Pio Gama Pinto's memory with Amilcar Cabral Mausoleum, located inside military headquarters in Guinea-Bissau, a clear demonstration that those who assassinated Cabral feared him in life and in death. Cabral was one of the greatest Africa revolutionary intellectuals and freedom fighters. He was assassinated before the dawn of Guinea-Bissau independence.

Firoze Manji has argued that 'Memorials are more about the future than they are about the past'.[1] Thus, so long as our people lack the basic need food, housing, education and human dignity, the grave of Pio Gama Pinto and Amilcar Cabral will continue being the memory of the future generation of freedom fighters and revolutionary shrine hope that spark resistance against imperialism and struggle for social justice and human rights in Kenya and Africa.

On February 24, 2021, it was 56 years since Pio Gama Pinto was assassinated. Comrades from Mathare Social justice Centre and the Revolutionary Socialist league and Ukombozi Library gathered again at the Pio Gama Pinto grave for reflections, reading poems, engaging in political education and book reading in memory of Pinto as we forged organic intellectuals for the liberation struggles. We reflected on the internationalists

---

1. Manji F and Bill Fletcher Jr (2013): Claim No Easy Victories: The Legacy of Amilcar Cabral. Dakar: CODESRIA / Daraja Press

who continue to inspire our community struggles and resistance against the neoliberal economy and imperialism, that has continued to dehumanize our people in Kenya and Africa a struggle that Pinto planted seeds of resistance through Mau Mau Movement and Pan Africanism.

Pio Gama Pinto was a great political organizer and thinker for Mau Mau liberation movement. The Pan African Movement, in its formative stages of Africa's liberation movement, Pinto played great role in resource mobilization and helping to set up organizations to ground freedom struggle with Pan-African perspectives. Through his writings, memorandums and letters to comrades and international solidarity networks, Pinto amplified the struggles of Mau Mau and Pan Africanism. Pinto was well-read and active in the international solidarity movement of Black People in the USA and he was in contact with great revolutionary Black people in the struggle such as Malcom X. And when Malcom visited Kenya in 1959, he was hosted by Pinto in his house in Westland. Together they planned on how to unify the Pan–African Movement with Black people struggle against racism and police violence in USA. Pio Gama Pinto was also instrumental in fundraising for air tickets for Patrice Lumumba, to travel to Ghana in 1958, during the All African Conference that was organized by Kwame Nkurumah for Africa liberation movement. The seeds of Pan–African Movement and Africa Union was sowed in the all African conference,

Pinto was great Pan–Africanist and freedom fighter for Africa that today is remembered more in Pan African movement internationally than in his home country Kenya. Hence the title of the book, *Kenya's Unsung Martyr* where his contribution and sacrifice, historical role was obscured by Jomo Kenyatta regime which betrayed the freedom struggle, and created economic model of capitalism which manifest in poverty and homelessness, police killings and hunger, as symbolized in the lives of people in Mathare, the home in which Pinto planted seeds of resistance through the Mau Mau Movement.

The spark that Pio Gama Pinto bore today inspires a new generation of social justice activist such as Mathare Social Justice Centre, which continues with the struggle of Mau Mau and of the ambitions of Pio Gama Pinto, the struggle for land, education and housing, and dignified life. We learn great lessons from Pio Gama Pinto that it's important to build a political instrument like a social justice movement, a political Party with ideological clarity. As a socialist, as part of nurturing and building cadres for the political struggle, Pinto was committed to this. He was part of formation of Kenya Study circle in early 1950s that were the seeds of political organizing, during the embryonic development of nationalist political movement under Kenya

African Union. The Study circle organically linked the political parties, trade unions and social organizations.

These are great political lessons for youth in Kenya to learn as to fight against ethnic mobilization and politics of hate and bankrupt of ideas. The social justice movement and Community Social Justice Centers must learn these lessons. Pio Gama Pinto's political philosophy and socialist theory must be the basis for study cells in community social justice centers as part of political education and grounding the movement cadres with ideological clarity and as part of building a class consciousness to members of the movement. This is the greatest homage that we can bestow to the great martyr of Kenya freedom struggle, Pio Gama Pinto.

Pio Gama Pinto also helped to set up Lumumba Institute as part of a political school for ideological training for cadres of the political movement, As political movements and Social Justice Centre Working Group, we must learn about the struggle and history of Pio Gama Pinto in grounding our social justice movement, with ideological clarity, commitment, establishing permanent political basic structure in the grassroots that can root the movement for democratic state in Kenya. These must be founded on social justice, a generation of alternative political leadership with solid foundation for the next 50 years as we were advised by Comrade Adwok Nyamba, the freedom fighter from Sudan liberation movement SPLA, He gave a lecture at the Mathare Social Justice Centre hall in 2020 on the challenges of liberation movement in Africa in the last 50 years of Africa independence, the pitfalls of Kenya liberation struggle and the failure to build political organization with ideological base, which was halted after assassination of Pio Gama Pinto. What was created was neocolonial communal violence, divisive ethnic politics, corruptions that breeds social injustices and human rights violations since independence.

The social justice movement must intensify our community struggle in building social justice centers with cadres that have developed working class consciousness and dedication as Pio Gama Pinto selflessness. We must read widely about our history of resistance and of the betrayals, to be able to anchor our movement in the path of building a democratic state in Kenya with the dream of Pio Gama Pinto of socialism as part of social justice and human rights, and hence the spark of Pinto bore lives in our struggle and our memory.

> *Pinto's family had deep roots in both India and Kenya. Rosario's daughter, Audrey Da Gama, said in a recent interview: 'My grandfather, Anton Filipe Da Gama Pinto, worked for the British civil*

service in Nyeri, Kenya, from 1919 to 1941. Pinto, Sevigne and my dad were born in Kenya, but educated in India.'

REFLECTION 4: KINUTHIA NDUNG'U

Czech author Milan Kundera wrote that the struggle against power was the struggle of memory against forgetting. Undermining memory is a well-known tactic of the oppressor. The book *Pio Gama Pinto, Kenya's Unsung Martyr* counters the imperialist conspiracy to silence the achievements of one of our liberation heroes.

Contributions in that book tell the story of the class nature of the Kenyan society. The contradictions between reactionary and progressive forces. The book exposes the international socio-economic, political and economically unjust capitalist system that shatters economies in the name of imperial hegemony. Comrade Pinto saw the liberation struggle as an attempt to overthrow the oppressive system of domination and exploitation. He made a very clear stand on what should happen after independence. We are introduced to a man with capacity for ideological clarity, mass organization, organizational discipline and commitment to the struggle. Not only did he talk the talk but walked the talk.

Franz Fanon writes that the role of the African petty bourgeoisie in the international capital has always been that of compradors. Amilcar Cabral in *Weapon of Theory* wrote of the historic responsibility of the petty bourgeoisie. In the colonial context, he writes, they could be called revolutionary while other sectors retain the doubts characteristic of their class or ally themselves to colonialists to defend their social status. Durrani's book gives us the historical context in which Pinto lived. A statement by the last Governor of Kenya confirmed Britain's support for Kenyatta since he belonged to the moderate camp that supported the status quo. This class became the domestic bulwark of imperialist plunder. They overturned the objective of the liberation struggle. Pinto and his fellow radical petty bourgeoisie comrades chose to side with the makers of history and oppose the successors of the home guards sustained by neocolonialism. He points out that the struggle had been a two-line struggle, either capitalism with rich getting richer and the masses poorer, or socialism with justice and equality.

Most importantly, Pinto took an ideological stand concerning the liberation struggle. He suffered detention for his role in formation of anti-imperialist East African Trade Union Congress. He was clear that the struggle against imperialism was struggle against colonialism as well as class struggle. He took up the banner of socialism, returned to class struggle and sought organizational forms to put ideology into practice. This is seen with the formation of Lumumba Institute to train KANU cadres and make the party a socialist organization with the end goal of making Kenya follow the socialist path.

Pinto was a man with great understanding of the struggle he was engaged in. He analyzed the material conditions of regular people. He was thus able to expose tribalism as a systemic colonial construct that arose out of material conditions and colonial influences. His analysis also enabled him correctly to understand the economic situation of the country. When imperialist puppets presented the reactionary CIA document, Sessional Paper no. 10 of 1965, charting a capitalist path, Pinto prepared a counter socialist policy paper articulating development of socialism in post-independence Kenya.

Counter revolutionary forces and their imperialist masters felt so threatened that they decided to silence him, to silence the pursuit for humanity, the struggle for socialism. This is the cancer of betrayal that Cabral addressed during Asagyefo Kwame Nkurumah's burial. Cabral warned that the cancer of betrayal had to be rooted out of Africa if we really wanted to crush imperialist domination.

Pinto's ideological profundity and fidelity to socialist principles is an inspiration to the generation of revolutionary workers and youths in our country. It is a reminder to cadres engaged in mass work of the importance of ideological development of the masses to ensure permanence of the revolution, to stand for active ideological struggle because it is the weapon for ensuring unity within our organizations in the interest of our struggle. The workers and youths of today must question the direction the county has taken since independence and use the great historical experiences to advance the working people vision of socialism.

If he has been extinguished yet there arise a thousand beacons from the spark he bore.

Suluhu ni Usoshialisti![1]

---

1. The solution is Socialism!

REFLECTION 5: MINOO KYAA

On February 24, 1965, Kenya experienced its first political assassination after independence. The life of Pio Gama Pinto was cut short by the colonial system which had already acquired a black face. Before his assassination, the British had already tried to silence him by detaining him. His father died while he was still in prison and was not allowed to attend the burial. This broke him down.

The life of Malcolm X was taken away three days before Pinto was assassinated. The two comrades believed in socialism and although Malcolm X was a Black nationalist, Pinto had managed to influence him to become a Pan-Africanist. The imperialist system could not allow this to continue happening for the two comrades had made great connection and were dedicated to the struggle of the people. Together, Pinto and Malcolm X formed an alliance based upon the suffering of Black Americans and Africans and planned to charge the USA with human rights violation at the United Nations.

Pinto's death was among the many political assassinations in Kenya that have gone unpunished, especially during the Kenyatta and Moi regimes which carried out massacres and assassinations as a calculated method to maintain themselves and their class in power. This tradition has continued to date; the neocolonial system does not take criticism on its ruthless policies that have continued to cause economic exploitation and social inequality due to the class struggle that Pinto recognized. He preached socialism to the people and its benefits and did not give up in trying to make Kenya a socialist state.

Pio Gama Pinto made great contributions towards the liberation struggle of Kenya. He went as far as learning Kiswahili for easy communication. He worked behind the scenes in every organization he was involved in so as to strengthen its structures and make it more efficient and effective. He worked closely with the Land and Freedom Army (Mau Mau) fighters that were led by Field Marshall Kimathi Waciuri who was arrested and hanged inside Kamiti Maximum Security prison by the colonial government on February 18, 1957. Many of the soldiers were also killed during the war in the forest. Despite all this, the freedom fighters, with the help of Pinto, did not relent: they continued to fight as Pinto went ahead and armed the freedom fighters in their hide-outs. He also worked closely with the freedom fighters' families and provided them with food and necessary information. Getting inspiration from the Russian revolution, the Mau Mau as a radical movement moved from the peaceful approach of petitioning the colonial activities to the armed struggle having realized that non-violent constitutional agitation had serious limitations. Many of these freedom fighters were assassinated and others put behind bars. Pinto looked for lawyers to help in these cases and started publications to expose the colonial government for killing and looting the people's properties while blaming it on the Mau Mau to discredit the movement. He made sure all the news went out to avoid monopolization of media houses by the imperialists; without Pinto reporting it would have been impossible to understand all the struggles of the people. The neocolonial system has refused to recognise Pinto as a Mau Mau freedom fighter and it is upon the future generation to re-write history until we have the complete Mau Mau history researched and written. That is when full contributions of Pinto in the struggle shall be well known.

Ideological groundings, strong organization and committed leadership were the main weapons to win against the imperialist war according to Pinto. He saw the need for grounding cadres since the colonial system was trying to prove to people that there were no other options apart from capitalism. Pinto went ahead and acquired funds to set up a political school, the Lumumba Institute to ground party cadres of KANU and mobilize the people to ensure that the ideology was put in place. Socialism started to get a lot of support and it was clear that capitalism is a system to oppress people since it created classes and wouldn't be able to make its profit unless there were a class of people frustrated enough to sell their labor. It was thus important for the colonial government to end the life of Pinto before socialism could take over and before people well understood class struggle. His views were very clear; he had a clear political understanding and social consciousness. Pinto expressed himself as a socialist through his actions and writings. He lived by his principles and died by his principles. Kenyatta later closed down Lumumba institute after they had killed Pinto.

Pinto dedicated his life towards the liberation struggle of the people. His life was unfortunately cut short by the imperialist system. This however motivates us to continue with the struggle because if we do not carry on with the class struggle, we shall continue to languish in poverty. We must understand that Uhuru must truly mean freedom for the people to be free of exploitation and poverty. Uhuru must be Uhuru for the masses.

REFLECTION 6: LEE-ANNE KAARI NDEGWA

Anti-Colonialism and the Struggle for African Liberation: A Call to Action

Most of our past leaders have been assassinated by imperialist forces because they feared the true freedom of the Black man, the freedom which Pio Gama Pinto died fighting for. The book, *Pio Gama Pinto: Kenya's Unsung Martyr* comprehensively touches on the phases of the life lived by Pio, his motivations, history, his involvement in trade unions and most importantly his political identity and consciousness. As a young man not yet known to the world from Goan origins, of Kenyan descent, Pio Gama Pinto would take the world by storm and live to be remembered as a political activist, trade unionist, political organizer, revolutionary journalist and most importantly an ally of the masses. Pio Gama Pinto was a man whose consciousness was awoken by the suffering of his people. He was a visionary, a man of action, he easily saw that western colonialism was seriously undermining the African social infrastructure based on traditional humanistic values. His views were shared by the like of Julius Nyerere, Amilcar Cabral, Frantz Fanon, Aimé Cesaire and Sekou Touré who saw that the best way to fight imperialism in their respective countries and in the African continent at large was to take up arms, equip themselves with knowledge, garner global experience and fight until all foreign domination was eliminated. Ironically, silencing the voice of Pio Gama Pinto only made it grow louder.

His involvement in campaigns that included the struggles of peasants against the British for the acquisition of large tracks of lans, which had begun from early 1920s, was just but one of his notable achievements that uniquely stood out. His role in the struggle of land has influenced environmental activist of today. It is mind-boggling that many of the modern-day capitalists are still at it, same form of environmental injustices on peasants who are not able to earn a dollar a day to just afford basic necessities. Land in Mathare, Kibera, Mukuru kwa Njenga and many other informal settlements are still witnessing such atrocities, and these are only within urban settlement areas, without mentioning the situation in rural areas. The need for revolutionary change in land issues in Kenya today continues to be a critical issue as this is a highly contested topic given the nature of the complexities that surround land-related conflicts.

It is incredible that Africa possessed such great minds such as Pio Gama Pinto who easily saw through the blinding smoke of colonization that its sole basis was to rob Africa of its wealth, a system of economic domination. Their progressive steps should not be side-lined but put at the forefront as Pio Gama Pinto was one of the great minds that engineered the Mau Mau Freedom Movement. With the rise in organized movements, the works, tactics, and history still dominate the literacy scene and materials being accessed across the African continent and in the diaspora. We see the desire of young Africa's to be heard, as they re-imagine a second liberation. Malcom X who was an ally to Pio Gama Pinto, had found great inspiration from Pio's work. It was his thinking that reshaped Malcom X thought on Black Nationalism to Pan Africanism when they interacted during his stay in Kenya in 1964. Like the political and social-economic tensions which influenced their times, they continue to shape the current conversation in today's time such as the Black Lives Matter movement.

What part then do you play in all this, I presume is your question? Have a look at your country, does capitalism rule in every sphere of life? Then clearly, we are not living the dream, that 'uhuru must be uhuru for the masses,' which was envisioned by the likes of Pio Gama Pinto and many other patriots in Africa. This book is a reminder that we need to hit the nail at the head, we need to address the elephant in the room as stated which is capitalism, a characteristic of a colonial empire in our African states, which are now headed by African leaders. Pinto lived and died addressing the internal struggles of the Kenyan people, why shouldn't we?

REFLECTION 7: GATHANGA NDUNG'U

It is quite hard being the good guy in a world that abhors the good people while treating the enemy hiding in a veneer with a lot of trepidation. If we were to judge the world history and how it has treated the good guy in development of our societies, its always the enemy flourishing. History has taught us that it's the Martin Luther Kings, the Dedan Kimathis, the Amilcar Cabral, the Thomas Sankaras and the Patrice Lumumbas who end up on the receiving end of the oppressor's barrel or sword while the Mobutu Sessekos, the Kenyattas and the Blaise Compaore continue to live happy lives after their clandestine, blood gushing dealings and engagements to keep power at all cost and acquire illicit wealth at the expense of poor majority. It is quite a contradiction and ironical in most of the scenarios where the people being fought for have in most instances helped the imperialists crucify and nail the same people helping them while in other cases watched as imperialist turned their arsenal on the good guys.

Life must be lived forward, nonetheless, it is the past that informs the decisions we make for the future.

Pio Gama Pinto: Kenya's Unsung Martyr tries to paint a very vivid picture on the life of one of Kenya's first post-independence martyr and his works, dreams and aspirations when the country was at crossroads on whether to take the capitalist route or the socialist path.

Reflections

The nexus between the Asian and Africans

At the age of eight years, Pinto was taken to India where he continued with his studies until he was seventeen. After that he acquired a job where he made good relation with the people of his origin. Coming back to Kenya helped him relate the problem Kenyans were facing with those of the Goan people back in India. From there, he drew conclusion that in order for the war on imperialists to be worn, the oppressed had to unite despite their different races, creed, nationalities and political affiliations just as the oppressors. The divide and rule method of colonialists had worked perfectly well in Kenya as the Asian communities had some privileges which made them to be on different social class with Africans. Rallying these two communities on a common goal was thus a problem. Pio was Asian and at the same time his DNA was screaming of the African he was deep down. Working on both sides with Africans and Asian on one side brought the two communities together and the war was finally between the oppressed and their oppressors. This would have not been the case as these two communities would have been turned against each other. Pinto was the silver cord of Indo-African relations.

An epitome of a true socialist

Pio Gama Pinto died trying to help people, he died a pauper as he spent his resources helping the vulnerable. He lived his daily life on his socialist maxim of equity and equality. He was the truest example of a socialist our nation has ever had. He had contextualised the African communities and the Kenyan to be specific. He believed that it was through socialism that our nascent nation would have achieved economic freedom and empowerment from the imperialists. Even in his detention in Manda Island, he never accepted any preferential treatment different from that of other Mau Mau detainees.

The strategist and tactician

A war is never won on one battlefront. Pio was alive to this fact and in his capacity he tried to wage his war on all possible fronts. From the publications on the broadsheets and other avenues as a journalist, to supporting financially and supplying food and guns to the Kenya Land and Freedom Army (KLFA) in the Aberdares and in the Mt. Kenya forest, to his links with trade unionists such as Makhan Singh and Fred Kubai and to mobilizing for pro-bono lawyers in courts to defend the Mau Mau fighters. He ran the cog to ensure all battlefronts were on high gear. As a newly-wed young man, he even lacked time for his family as he had put the liberation struggle as a personal priority. He made sure that the international community was informed on what was going on in Kenya through his contact persons in UK and other countries. This helped build pressure on the Britain Government from their parliament. All these factors of being a good tactician and strategist made him become an easy target for both the colonialist government and their successor post –independence government.

When things were tough for Joseph Murumbi, he organised for him to seek asylum in the UK as things cooled down. He kept him informed on the matters going on in the country.[1]

He was also regarded as the brain behind the works of the first Vice President of Kenya, Oginga Odinga.

The unambitious politician

With the current crop of politicians in Kenya, this might be baffling. Our politics are characterised by self-seeking, ambitious and selfish clout of politicians who put their interests first before their constituents. Pio worked seamlessly behind the curtains to ensure everything was done in time and in a professional way. He had no intentions of being in the lime light for any self-seeking ambitions. It was always the people first. His life was very political yet he had no any personal political ambitions. He even had to be forced to consider the elections to the Central Legislation Assembly slots in Parliament.

Pio: The Urban Guerrilla

Even though Pio was never in the forest with the KLFA, he was the urban field marshal juggling from one department to another all in ensuring that those in the forest had food and fire arms and that the families of freedom fighters were fine and that the detainees had lawyers to defend them. His own house would harbour people of all kinds, some in transit, while others seeking asylum and others strategizing on how to wage anti-colonial war in their own countries. He was always meeting people to strategize in his house over dinner and luncheons.

The Kenyan in Asian Skin

Pio was more Kenyan than many black Kenyans in the country at the time. While others were betraying their mother country and others giving the liberation war a lukewarm and a tentative approach, Pinto plunged head-first in the epicentre of all this even after being released from detention and restriction. His understanding of the Kenyan problems and commitment

---

1. Page 193 on Joseph Murumbi's memoir on 'Pinto; Nationalist and Freedom Fighter', There is a probably a typographical or an editing error. From the first paragraph, the chronology implies that Pio Gama Pinto was born in 1919 and in 1927 at the age of eight that's when he was taken to India. There are also errors due to memory where some of the individuals confused his town of restriction; Kabarnet with Kapsabet.

was unrivalled. Mau Mau was a very covert army and very closely knit and shrouded in secrecy. The oaths taken were to ensure that secrets never went out and that outsiders would not know the operation of this group. Despite the mistrust between the fighters and the home guards and the possible infiltrations by colonial sympathizers, Pio was very much trusted despite his skin pigmentation which would have otherwise disadvantaged him.

A Bud Nipped Before Blossom

February 24, 1965 shall forever be permanently embedded in the hearts and minds of every true African historian and any politically conscious citizen of Kenya. On the morning of this day, a bud was nipped before its blossom into one of the most beautiful flowers and the fruits that we shall never get to taste from this flower. His star rose steadily due to the dedication and commitment he had to the struggle of this country. The neocolonialists saw his dedication and commitment to the African course as a threat to their freedom to exploit other Africans. The colonialists saw his socialist ambitions as a threat to their imperialist hegemony and so it was to the best of both of their nefarious ambitions to nip the bud before it blossomed and diffused its fragrance to the whole nation and Africa as a whole. This would have rattled and challenged the status quo and probably tilting our nation to the socialist path. His dreams, aspirations and visions of a country free from exploitation with equity and justice were cut short at a very early stage. Nevertheless, the quality of life is not measured by the number of years one lives but the impact one makes. His political life was short spanning about 17 years yet was very impactful and we continue to enjoy some of his fruits till this day.

May his undying spirit be rekindled in us and may the ink of his indelible mark never dry or fade in us and the next generations to come.

REFLECTION 8: EZRA OTIENO

In his brief life, Pinto had become a voice of Kenyan and Indian anti-colonial and anti-imperialist movements. He was an early participant in Goa's anti-Portuguese colonial struggle as well as Mau Mau during Kenya's liberation war. From 1954 to 1959, he was imprisoned in Kenya by British colonial authorities. His commitment to the fight for working-class independence spanned various places of the world. He was a prolific author, but he stayed low-key. He believed he could do better by not competing in elections to join the bandwagon. This was a commitment to uncovering the injustices committed on innocent Africans who, while being politically knowledgeable, couldn't even express their complaints in the world's language. They became men who were frequently hampered by their failure to respond rhetorically to the complaints that came thick and hard, and instead had to resort to physical force in the end.

I learned about his unrelenting spirit of selflessness and the unimaginable lengths he went to help Mau Mau. Pinto was an important supplier in Nairobi for the Mau Mau, working with the Nairobi War Council to smuggle money, food, weapons, and classified info through the forests, and smuggling out of Kenya and then into the world's news accounts and images of security forces massacres before his activities were uncovered and he was captured. He was concerned that many of those who gave up their land, educational and other resources, bodies, or even live in the name of freedom be properly honored.

Pinto was also an arbitrator. He was primarily responsible for stopping the Mau Mau's vengeance from being directed at the Indian people. Vast numbers of Indians could have been slaughtered and their property stolen if he had not been able to join the underground conclaves of the freedom fighters unseen and if he'd never gained the confidence of members such as Jomo Kenyatta, Stanley Mathenge, Chief Koinange, and others for his sound and direct advice.

His rivals found no other way to put an end to his life-long suffering except with the assassin's bullets. However, his contribution, his thoughts, can never be erased from the people's hearts.

This book, *Pio Gama Pinto: Kenya's Unsung Martyr,* didn't attempt to be or pretend to be a detailed record of Pio Gama Pinto; rather, it is the beginning of the long journey needed to document Kenya's history from an anti-imperialist viewpoint. It exposes the voices of many people who have written about Pinto to provide the most accurate representation of Pinto possible. In that spirit, it aims to make history accessible to those whose stories it is—Kenyans, Africans, and revolutionary people all over the world.

The sacrifices of the hundreds of thousands of Kenya's freedom fighters must be honored by the effective implementation of the policy—a democratic, African, socialist state in which the people have the right to be free from economic exploitation and the right to social equality. Kenya's Uhuru must not be transformed into freedom to exploit, or freedom to be hungry and live in ignorance. Uhuru must be uhuru for the masses – uhuru from exploitation, from ignorance, disease, and poverty', he stated. He realized that the only way to honor the independence heroes was the implementation of socialism where workers could own the means of production.

Pinto was an excellent strategist. He secured massive funds for KANU without the knowledge of colonial forces which were wired to India from his communist contacts, then through Tanzania and finally to Kenya. He was very instrumental in the fight for independence in 1963. He did not contest in elections to maximize his efficiency. His quiet way of operations proved useful on many occasions. He was used to neutralize opposing organizations and he also helped fund progressive trade unions.

He was an ardent supporter of trade unions. Pinto looked up to Nkrumah and organized travels for he Ghanaian trade unionist, John Kofi Barku Tettegah, to come to Kenya and meet Kenyatta. He was very pleased to learn of the formation of the organization of African Trade unions in 1973 where Dennis Akumu was the secretary-general. His contact with Makhan Sigh and his support for that trade union was also a way he showed his solidarity. While in detention, Makhan Sigh received a book *The Outline of History* by H.G Wells, knowing the consequences of being caught.

Pinto would be shocked to find the present-day state of the workers, their wages, co-opted trade union leaders, and how the cost of living has risen. His deep concern about ordinary people made him envision a society where a human being could not be penalized for being underprivileged. He fought for economic development all over the country especially in less developed areas under colonial rule. He understood the exploitation by landlords in urban areas and pushed for rent control to cushion tenants. His role in advocating for free and universal healthcare was huge. He did the same for the education sector too. He brushed shoulders with elites who accumulated wealth at the expense of the proletariat. This was the genesis of the plot of his assassination. A true revolutionary in words and deeds.

His main principle was democracy, liberty and an equal chance for everyone. Kikuyu Central Association members who were detained with him spoke highly of him as a respectful person who treated everyone equally. As Odinga quoted in one of his articles,' Anyone who met Pio soon forgot his pigmentation because his works and deeds left no doubt that he was a Kenyan nationalist.' All the money he gathered for the liberation struggle was accounted for to the last coin. He was not a deceitful man. The money he got was used for its intended purpose. As the secretary of the Pan African press, he earned fifty pounds. He told his wife he earned twenty-five pounds. The rest, he gave to the poor.

On the day of his death, people from all walks of life streamed into his home; the poor, friends, people he had helped, and his fellow detainees. This showed what kind of person he was. The burial which took place the next day saw multitudes of people streaming in for the burial some even heading to the wrong venues. This response was unbelievable and is one of the most memorable sendoffs people have been accorded. The respect people accorded him will forever remain in the history books.

Even in his death, his socialist friends stayed loyal and true to him and his beliefs. They defied government directives and even raised funds in Pinto's name. Notable names who contributed were, Fitz de Souza, Julius Nyerere, Achieng Oneko among others. This helped his family who now settled in Canada.

Comrade Pinto is away from us today because of the bullets of vicious killers. We wish he was there to continue with the fight but we are here to keep his memories alive. The ideals which he sacrificed and worked for must continue with the current generation to honor him. His light should never dim. It should continue to shine a light to the darkness in society. His dedication and sincerity to the struggle is something to be admired.

Long live the spirit of Comrade Pio!

REFLECTION 9: DAVIS TAFARI

The liberation struggle never stops, every revolutionary has a role to play to make sure that everyone lives in an equitable society free of any kind of violence because the greater the fairness between the people the more human dignity is respected in all measures and as a result a nation prospers. The conditions set by colonialism still dominate to date as majority of the people are living in deplorable conditions, young men are killed daily in the Informal settlements as it was during colonial period and excessive force is used against unarmed citizens during protests against the dominance of neoliberalism

Every revolutionary has a duty to play in every front of liberation struggle by all means possible for the interest of workers and the outcome reward should be liberation for the majority and not individual gain.

Reflection: Pinto—The Radical Journalist

Pinto was a Goan-Indian Kenyan born on March 31, 1927. He was sent to India for his education by his father and from his earliest age Pio Gama Pinto was a rebel. In 1944, he joined the Indian air force for a briefly as a clerk before taking a job with the post and telegraph company in Bombay. While still in Goa he was among the founder of Goan National Congress whose aim was to liberate Goa from the yoke of Portuguese colonial rule. It is this experience that he came back with and used it in every aspect on the Kenya's liberation struggle.

He took part in the formation of radical trade union movements, progressive political and learning institution like the Patrice Lumumba Institute as well as publishing and popularizing socialist politics and policies. He was also active in the Mau Mau armed struggle by supplying guns, medical, cash and other support to fighters of the Mau Mau when it became obvious that organized armed struggle was needed for liberation.

While Pinto was still in the Indian air force where he spent 18 months, he studied journalism, which he used to unify other aspects of the struggles he was active in. He used journalism as a way to combat colonial government propaganda by editing newsletters and articles in different languages and assisted in the publication of anti-government African newsletters together with his team. In 1952, Pinto and other patriots like Ambu Patel began a publication to expose the cowardly and cruel action of the colonial government

In this line of work, Pinto realized the Importance of teamwork. He helped young newspapermen who used to publish broadsheets those days and because journalism needed resources, Pinto helped the young journalists by buying them papers, printing machines and even supporting them financially. While working in Asian Congress office he used skills to type broadsheets for them. However, the broadsheets were very radical that the colonial government banned them from the public.

Pio Gama Pinto saw a need to develop a communication strategy for the anti-colonial liberation forces because it was a good way to combat colonial and post-colonial attacks on its organization, leadership and radical ideology. Pinto together with his left-wing comrades saw the need of coming up with independent press as a channel of communication. Pinto participated in printing and distribution of anti-colonial posters and leaflets. It was necessary for any liberation forces in Kenya to counter the new imperialist onslaught with a more powerful media strategy. Pinto knew the power of the press in the distribution of information, he went to India in 1960 to ask for funds to help establish KANU press which he was given by the then firsts prime minister of India, Jawaharlal Nehru. That brought the birth of *Pan African Press* in 1961. The Press published articles such as *Sauti ya Kanu* and the *Pan African*. Pio Gama Pinto was the editor for both. Although, he was a good role model as a journalist and a prolific writer, he seemed to prefer to operate behind the curtains. He never looked for personal credit. He used to work with a team of dedicated progressive like-minded socialists like Bildad Kaggia, Senior chief Koinange and the Mau Mau Activists tirelessly to make the dream of a socialist state a reality.

Pio Gama Pinto was a brilliant strategist in Oginga Odinga's camp. He was able to link different aspects of the struggle and ensure the togetherness of all progressives to strengthen the overall anti-imperialist struggle, even when he was arrested and detained in 1954 in Takwa detention camp on Manda island five months after his wedding to Emma Gama pinto, and later he was restricted at Kabarnet until October 1959. Thereafter he continued with his journalism work and his revolutionary activity. He was fearless and never afraid to annoy and embarrass colonial authorities.

Together with his progressive team, Pio Gama started a counter propaganda move to restore the morale of the detainees who were giving up and giving in to colonial propaganda that was demoralizing them. While in detention he played a very big role in a well-organized network as the editor of the propaganda. His anti-imperialism stand is seen through his writings that have survived like, *Glimpses of Kenya's Nationalist Struggle* among others. His writings made him to be considered an enemy of the colonialist and the comprador group in the government. Pinto concern was for the ordinary person. His concern was not in favor of the ruling classes or their imperialist backers but rather for the worker and the quest for a revolutionary change to combat the historical imbalances imposed by colonialism. Pinto worked tirelessly to undress the well-dressed lies of imperialism and neo-colonialism.

Although Pinto did not have the powerful backing of the government, his journalism and activism gave him power beyond the government influence. Through his independent press he had influence in public opinion and this did not go well his enemies who plotted to assassinate him.

President Jomo Kenyatta felt threatened by Pinto and the group associated with him led by Oginga Odinga who opposed the move of Kenyatta and his trusted loyalists to take over lands acquired back from the colonialists who had been defeated by Kenyan's resistance to colonialism. Further this was a continuation to entrench the imperialist interests at the expense of Kenyan citizen. Pinto together with his team planned an action and drafted a parallel paper that was to counter the *Sessional Paper Number 10* which the comprador government was going to introduce in parliament. Odinga was the one to introduce the counter version of African socialism which was radically different from the government.

The comprador government saw this as a real threat and sought to suppress the voice of Pio Gama Pinto by eliminating him. He was killed a few days before the parliamentary sitting, it was clear that the radical paper that Pio Gama Pinto had prepared would expose Kenyatta government evilness. Pinto being the architect of the move was assassinated. His assassination put an end to the introduction of the alternative paper in parliament. Pinto used Journalism as a tool to combat capitalism really worked in his favor. The neocolonial government employed the tactics of using media to brainwash the society and it is still using media to push government interest and shape the narratives.

REFLECTION 10: NICHOLAS MWANGI

There is no absence of ideology in our history. There is only its suppression and attempted erasure.
— Pheroze Nowrojee, in *Pio Gama Pinto: Kenya's Unsung Martyr 1927-1965.*

February 24, 2021 marked the 56th anniversary of the assassination of Pio Gama Pinto, a revolutionary socialist and an advocate of social justice and equality. To honor the memory and the ideals that Pio Gama Pinto stood for, two activities were held in Nairobi to reflect on the contributions of Pio Gama Pinto in the Kenyan struggle. One event took place at the Pio Gama Pinto memorial grave at City Park on February 25, 2021, where young people including activists and community organizers held a reflection session on his contributions to the struggle for social justice and socialism in Kenya. The other activity has been ongoing and is the *Pio Gama Pinto podcast* now on its fourth episode produced by April Zhu and Stone face Bomba, it is done in Sheng, a language that easily resonates with young people. The podcast has become a popular source of history by providing clarity on the rather obscure struggles of Pio Gama Pinto. The podcast crew also organized another event at Cheche bookshop on February 28, 2021 where attendants were given a chance to hear the first episode in honor of Pio Gama Pinto.

Pinto Memorial Grave

The memory of Pio Gama Pinto has been kept alive through young people in Kenya agitated by massive corruption through subsequent governments since independence. Mass unemployment, international debts running into trillions, inequality and privatization of key sectors such as health and education has greatly affected the livelihoods of Kenyans. Kenya finds itself in a complete crisis with growing hopelessness among its citizens. These post-colonial challenges are rooted in the transition politics of independence by African elite who betrayed the people of Kenya that fought for political and economic freedom for their country. The capitalist crisis today was forewarned by Pio Gama Pinto in 1963 when he said;

Kenya's Uhuru must not be transformed into freedom to exploit, or freedom to be hungry and live-in ignorance. Uhuru must be Uhuru for the masses, Uhuru from exploitation, from ignorance, disease and poverty. (1963)

Pio Gama Pinto envisioned such a society and worked tirelessly for it to become a reality. Certainly, we would have had a different society if his ideas were embraced and laid the foundation for independent Kenya. But, enemies of equality and justice decided to put an end to his vision through an assassin bullet in 1965. The life of Pio Gama Pinto makes a solid case for socialism in Kenya. Those who believed and fought for an alternative system to capitalism. The life and times of Pio Gama Pinto is that of a selfless, courageous and visionary individual.

Kenya as a country has never recovered from this betrayal. After the death of Pio Gama Pinto capitalism was presented as a natural system to the masses with no alternative to it. The imperialists through the independence government hoodwinked the people of Kenya through a CIA inspired document known as *African Socialism* published in 1965 to calm the growing agitation against capitalism and imperialism. This was not a socialist document but a capitalist blueprint in disguise designed to counter the real socialists and progressives in Kenya. *The Wananchi declaration: The Programme of the Kenya People's Union.* published in 1965 is what Pinto was part of, exposed the trickery of the 'African Socialism' document, in its scientific analysis it asserts;

> *Under the cloak of something called 'African Socialism', Kenya is moving towards one of the more orthodox forms of capitalism to be in the world today. Why does the KANU government call its policy socialism, and not dare admit that it follows the capitalist road? Because it knows well that capitalism is utterly wrong and unsuited to the needs and the aspirations of the people of Kenya*

Capitalism was reborn and manifested itself on African 'elite' leaders. Kenya was moving towards being a neocolonial state. The likes of Pio Gama Pinto saw the danger of this and exposed the power of imperialism and capitalism beyond color. The white capitalist was 'leaving' and was being replaced with a black capitalist who would serve us a puppet to the interest of imperialism. Walter Rodney best describes this in *How Europe Underdeveloped Africa:*

> *... but a black man ruling a dependent State within the imperialist system has no power. He is simply an agent of the whites in the*

metropolis, with an army and a police force designed to maintain the imperialist way of things in that particular colonial area.

Proponents of socialism like Pio Gama Pinto had gone beyond Pan Africanism and nationalism which was the wave in Africa at the time and dominated post-colonial politics. He applied scientific class analysis on the society and exposed the class nature/composition in Kenya. As Shiraz, puts it: 'He exposed colonialism, imperialism and capitalism'.

This analysis was important because it was the politics of nationalism that elevated Jomo Kenyatta and other elites. They were able to use Pan Africanism as an ideology towards achieving their interests and solidify capitalism system in Kenya. Self-African rule under capitalism did not mean that every Kenyan was going to benefit from the fruits of independence in terms of getting their land back, jobs, health care and education or control of their economy, capitalism actually does the opposite and Pinto understood that, and for that they killed him.

Although they killed him, they could not kill his ideas and neither could they kill the efforts of those who were inspired by his struggles and tirelessly researched and wrote on Pio Gama Pinto. This book that we are reflecting on *Pio Gama Pinto: Kenya Unsung Martyr 1927-1965* compiled by Shiraz Durrani, is the sweat and effort for over the last thirty years. Capitalism and imperialism thrive in any society by erasing the memory and history of those who are critical of it. Our Neo-liberal education model defined its own heroes while demeaning or removing all together revolutionaries and those who fought for this country. Ngugi Wa Thiong'o writes in *Never Be Silent: Publishing & Imperialism in Kenya 1884-1963* by Shiraz Durrani.

> Information is power in war and peace. But information, particularly in the struggle between the dominated and the dominating, is never neutral. The dominating try to control the sources, agents and contents of information.

In an article written by Wainaina Wambui on the standard paper on October 14, 2018, while reflecting on this book; further highlights how Pinto was reduced to a footnote in our schools:

> *Any product of the Kenyan school system will remember the striking image of a handsome man of Indian origin as they flipped through their history books. But beyond curriculum duty, past newspaper, magazine and scattered online articles, one is hard-pressed to find writings, ideas and a detailed record of the life of Pio Gama Pinto,*

the charismatic person who became independent Kenya's first political martyr. — Nicholas Mwangi and Shiraz Durrani, *2018*

As we remember Pio Gama Pinto, the revolutionary hero embedded in the people struggles, we also celebrate and acknowledge Shiraz Durrani for this magnificent work. This book will continue to teach and expose generation after generation of young people to the fine politics, ideas and beliefs of Pio Gama Pinto whom the government of Kenya has long wished to erase from our memories. Shiraz first wrote on Pio Gama Pinto in 1984 on *The Standard* newspaper. After the publication of the article, the special branch police begun monitoring him and Shiraz had to relocate to London for safety. However, this did not deter him from continuing to gather material on Pio Gama Pinto and thirty-four years later after the first article in 1984, *Pio Gama Pinto book; Kenya unsung Martyr 1927-1965* was published in 2018.

REFLECTION 11: BRIAN MATHENGE

Pio Pinto: A Life in Struggle

I would have wanted to engage with Pinto, write letters, interact in struggle, and exchange ideas, but I will dedicate these reflections of his works as a mirror and guide to the character of our struggle, and principles of our lives to all fighters of social justice.

> *If he has been extinguished, yet there arise a thousand beacons, from the spark he bore.*

March 31, 1927, brought a historic significance with it, there rose a fighter and a great defender for economic and social justice. He became a symbol of resistance and hope for the new Kenya. He studied and spent his early life in India, participated in working class struggles which prepared him for future tasks. Then, we have a Kenyan republic that is rebuilding from the colonial struggles, an independent Kenya that ought to decide and forge its independent path, though clouded with contradictions from the selfishness and thirst for power of the petty bourgeois.

Pio Gama Pinto, a radical African-Asian, with a committed revolutionary course, and a clear Political trajectory emerged in the capital of Kenya, Nairobi, and lived ahead of his time. His revolutionary ideals remain intact, absorbed into history. Every progressive force owes up to the contributions of our forefathers, to continue with the liberation course and support struggles of the oppressed everywhere.

Kenya, a former British colony, was going through a delicate transition from colonialism to independence by the time he was killed. Kenyan struggles against British colonialism, started with a wave of resistance from underground movements in Africa, shook the colonial rule. In Kenya, the Land and Freedom Army was blazingly organizing the Kenyans against the British, sending uncomfortable heat, challenging the British occupation. Pio was instrumental in organizing, and coordinating underground resistance and mobilizing resources for the fighters.

Being a family man, a husband to Emma Cristine, and a father, he gave up his roles for the Liberation of the masses, at one point arrested in 1954, just five months after marrying Emma, and detained in Takwa and Manda island. The *Sessional Paper No.10 on African Socialism*, was the document that caused the tragic systematic murder of Pio at his home. A retrogressive document that has caused all the suffering and the continued misery, the ever-growing economic inequality in Kenya. The foundation document that through the USA government became practicalized and effected, it advocates for private ownership of land, provides for strengthening foreign relationships, rather than an economic break-up with the foreign powers and proposes 'progressive' taxation of its citizens without a development approach.

> Kenya Uhuru must not be transformed into freedom to exploit, or freedom to be hungry and live-in ignorance. Uhuru must be Uhuru for the masses. Uhuru must be Uhuru for the masses, Uhuru from ignorance, disease and poverty.— Pio Pinto

Pio stood for socialism and he was there when the working-class struggles called, he took a clear ideological stance on matters pressing the nation. He stood against the systematic oppression by imperialists, then, colonialism. Having participated consistently, in the struggles against British and Portuguese colonialism both in Kenya and India, he was instrumental in formation of the Goa National Congress, the Mau Mau War Council in Mathare, the Kenya African Union, they even took a house with Fitz De Souza to facilitate organizing the defence of six detainees. He was specific and clear that the urgent matter, in history, then, and now, is the class struggle. He believed that the only way to achieve freedom was through workers owning the means of production. His role in organizing the trade unions, workers' strikes and boycotts in a very decisive period in history, suggests that Pinto understood the power of the organization of workers and the economic structure, that was the source of inequality. Workers are still subjected to harsh conditions to date, despite the potential power they hold it has not been capitalized due lack of an organization with ideological theory

The book details an experience of hope, courage and an avowed commitment to the liberation struggle. It grows the desire to live the ideals of Pinto, to fight and use Marxism as a science to transform our society.

Apart from being a key strategist, aiding and sourcing arms for the underground movements in Kenya, the Kenya Land and Freedom Army, he supported the Angolan, Mozambique, against Portuguese Colonialism, his contributions in Goa, projects the principle of working-class internationalism. In Parliament, he stood unshaken on ideological positions. He became a threat to the former home guards in the old Kenyan society, who reaped benefits from colonial masters, and were then protecting the interests of colonial masters.

When the Sessional Paper was being introduced in the floor of the house, a documet that would determine the foundation of a new Kenya, imposed by the western imperialist powers, Pinto had lobbied for the rejection of the document. He had disturbed the pigs' peace, and there was discomfort among the pigs' camp.

On February 24, 1965, Pinto was shot outside his house in the presence of her daughter, by three armed men. He had foreseen his death. A few days after the murder of Malcolm X, a Black Liberation activist, who, upon visiting Kenya, was inspired by Pio Gama Pinto, was shot on February 21, 1965. Exposing the cowardice of the Imperialist apparatus. His death spread a sad, and tragic moment for Kenya. Being the first martyr in independent Kenya, he was greatly loved and admired figure. His burial was attended massively, by top, influencial people. Both houses adjourned in honor of his memory. Oginga Odinga and Joseph Murumbi, Aching Oneko mourned deeply.

We celebrate and emulate his life today, a new generation of resistance inspired by his life has risen among organizations.

The shutting of Lumumba Institute was an exposition of his killers. It is clear that ideological clarity is important, ideological theory is an important weapon in our daily battles, to the social injustice system. It is also very important to carry and preserve the interests of the masses at heart, and hold strongly to our ideology, Marxism, as a science to transform our society. When I told Comrade Willy Mutunga about the reflections, he wrote:

> Please go to City Park, (to his grave) . Gacheke can take you there. Quote the words on headstone.

This is the quote:

> Our heroines and heroes are not in their graves. Their revolutionary Spirits are the equivalent of the Holy Spirit. They live within us.

REFLECTION 12: ANTONY ADOYO

Kenya's struggle for independence was one that inspired other countries struggle for independence from colonial rule. Pinto was instrumental in Kenya's liberation struggle as he was in many different fronts at the same time. My first visit to his grave site was heart breaking because for a cadre who played an instrumental role in the liberation struggle his memory and grave have been neglected.

Pinto was a selfless fighter, evidenced by his deeds. The book documents that when he left prison, he gave out his shoes to fellow inmates who did not have shoes. He also used a huge part of his salary as member of parliament, to take care of the families of fellow freedom fighters. His involvement in the liberation struggles of Kenya and India and his international link with Malcom X, shows that he was an internationalist and was not defined by race. He saw colonialism and imperialism as human and world problems and not race.

Pinto's contribution to Kenya's liberation struggles is unmatched to date. He was dedicated and with a desire to see Kenya free from exploitation and poverty. He was also committed to ideological studies and this led him to establish the Lumumba Institute that was meant to ground cadres of KANU political party. His intentions were pure but the majority of those who surrounded him were driven by private accumulation of wealth. Drawing from his example we must therefore strengthen the current Thomas Sankara Political School, to ideological cadres of emerging movements and to unite the left wing in Kenya.

The Kenyan left wing today has not lived up to the foundations that were set by Pinto and his generation on the liberation of our people. We are divided and are constantly on battles of superiority and whose struggle is better than the other. There is no link between older generations of leftist and the new generations that are coming up as they have been left alone to find their own path. It is full of academic braggadocio on who has read Karl Marx more than the other instead of mentoring the upcoming young generations of leftists.

Rather than to wage struggles on too many fronts, it is time to form a united front with a clear political program gear towards the economic liberation of our people, to honour the memory of Pio Gamma Pinto.

Today's generation of political activists, community organizers and left-wing cadres can learn a lot from Pio Gamma Pinto as the first Social Justice Martyr.

Today the biggest challenge that lies ahead is to form a unifying socialist party that will spearhead the third liberation struggle for the economic liberation of our country. In doing so we should put in mind the following excerpt from the book *Pio Gamma Pinto: Kenya's Unsung Martyr* by Shiraz Durrani.

> *In life, as in death, Pinto exposed the class nature of the Kenyan society. He exposed colonialism, imperialism and capitalism as the evils that the working people of Kenya needed to defeat. When it was time to write political and legal cases for people's rights, Pinto was there. When it was time to form strong political parties, Pinto was there. When it was time to develop working class and anti-imperialist ideologies, Pinto was there. When it was time to face the enemy with guns, Pinto was there. When it was time to support victims of colonial and neo-colonialism terrorism, Pinto was there. When it was time to take a political stand after independence, Pinto was there. When people in other countries in Africa and elsewhere needed support to fight colonial and capitalist exploitation and oppression, Pinto was there. When it was time to make personal and family sacrifices for a greater cause, Pinto was there. And when the end came, when it was time to stand for his principles and to die for his country, Pinto was there. It is rare to find all these qualities in one person.*

Once I read the book, to date I am always confronted with the qualities of Pinto documented in the above excerpt most especially when conducting self-criticism. The realities that I live in demand that I commit class suicide on a daily basis confronted with family demands and expectations. The task ahead of us also demands commitment and dedication. Driven by the desire to see my daughter Nina Illiana living in a world free from exploitation and oppression, I dedicate my life to the socialist struggle and revolution. Seeing the daily smiles of daughter, reminds me that the liberation and empowerment of women must be deliberate, consistent with socialist ideals and sustained because as Thomas Sankara said, 'there can be no true revolution without the true liberation of women.

Long live Socialism!

REFLECTION 13: MZALENDO WANJIRA

Pio Gama Pinto. Brave. Patriotic. Ideologically clear, uncompromising, unrelenting, a true freedom fighter! Freedom for our country, freedom for the people of Africa.

Socialism was always a strong part of the dreams Pio Gama Pinto had for Kenya. He was born in Kenya to Goan parents who were also first generation Goans born in Kenya Indeed for a long time he knew no other soil than this country and his nationalist views reflected this. It was clear he identified with the land and the people. Pinto studied in India between 1938 and 1947. He worked briefly in the army and telegrams office in India before going back to Kenya in 1949. As he continued to develop his political stance he was strongly against oppression and aligned himself with the people. This was the beginning of the push for social justice and equality in Kenya. Pinto was in fact, a committed social justice warrior. At age 17, Pinto protested against Goan oppression in Bombay by Portuguese colonialism; as a student, he had to leave India to return to Kenya to avoid arrest by Portuguese authorities. In Kenya he came face to face with British racism and class exploitation of the indigenous people. Fixated on the far but present hope of liberation. This must have been the mood as patriots incarcerated on Manda Island. Prisoners of the seemingly eternal struggle for truth, justice and rights. Operation Anvil with its biased hand had landed a great deal of otherwise innocent men and women behind bars in makeshift dungeons dotted across East Africa. This particular prison held Pio Gama Pinto who was a journalist chronicling and clandestinely supporting a guerrilla movement [Kenya Land and Freedom Army] demanding change and an end to colonialist aggression and occupation. The year is 1954 and the calls for the Union Jack [British Flag] to be lowered grew ever louder. They ached for Land. Liberation. Freedom to be and be with dignity.

Reflection

The Mau Mau are famous for the oathing ceremonies they conducted to recruit fighters into their revolutionary army. The ritual bonds the fighters in a similar way to the way ideological clarity unites cadres under a single purpose; the pursuit of justice. We may never know if Pinto participated in such an event but it is clear from his resolve that he was a man of principle and with a cause worth dying for. Thrusting himself into the political scene, he joined with Joseph Murumbi and Walter Odede to push for nationalism under the Kenya African Union (KAU). Pinto, the mental heavyweight, was a key component of the think tank of this party that would later become KANU. He was a man of many hats, a writer, journalist, radio presenter, trade unionist, editor, clerk who resigned from the *Daily Chronicle*, Congress posts and India Radio in 1951 to concentrate fully on the gathering storm that was the Kenyan liberation struggle. Pio Gama Pinto maintained a strong socialist ideology in his work. Recognizing the importance of land and its occupation he began to articulate this question diligently. He translated a 200-page Kikuyu Memorandum on land and forwarded grievances and excesses of the settler colonial regime to British MPs, especially after the arrest of the Kapenguria Six. To further proletarian propaganda newspapers were established called the *High Command* which Pinto was the editor in chief. At this, the colonial government arrested him and under heavy guard locked him up in Manda Island with hardcore Mau Mau comrades. They held him there for four years and a few months of isolation in Kabarnet. However, the battle for Kenya's independence had been won by the strong will of the Kenyan people. To date, Pio Gama Pinto remains one of the few Asians to be jailed during the war.

This was not the end as Pinto intensified his quest for regional liberation and the establishment of popular socialist regimes which he hoped would deliver the proletariat from exploitation. He returned to India in 1960 to support the Goan struggle against the Portuguese. While there he also began to identify with the struggle of Mozambique and especially with FRELIMO, which was fighting the vice of Portuguese aggression. He supported their struggle using the progressive government in Tanganyika (Tanzania). Pio alongside predecessors like Makhan Singh and Chege Kibachia fathered trade unions and their importance in levelling the workers' struggle is undisputed. Oftentimes I wonder to myself, what would the present Kenya look like had Pinto's ideas and dreams for Kenya materialized? That image, of a beautiful country, with equity and social justice, fuels my patriotism always.

While serving as an MP in Kenya's newly formed parliament, Pinto would fall out with Jomo Kenyatta and the State machinery regarding *Sessional Paper No 10*. Dr Fitz De Souza, who was also in parliament at the time, recounts a shouting contest in the halls of the caucus. Whether this took place or not, Pinto was obviously and vocally against the legalization of capitalism and the invitation to neo-colonialism that a young Kenya was heading to. Ego bruised and embarrassed the status quo had planned to eliminate Pinto to give way for their schemes to hijack Kenya's popular revolution. After meeting Malcolm X in Nairobi in 1959, the two discovered how much they had in common and Pinto had planned to go to the United Nations to decry the plight of black people in America.

In 1964, as deep contradictions began to appear in the top brass and Pinto increasingly began to disagree with the regime. He had worked on Soviet diplomacy that would see the creation of the Lumumba Institute to train Kanu Cadres. How revolutionary! Pio Gama Pinto was pushing for political education in 1964. This did not sit well with the corrupt members of the early cabinet and in 1965 Pinto was assassinated in full view of his young family in cold blood. According to an unpublished tribute by his younger brother, the late Rosario Da Gama Pinto, the killing was imminent: 'Pio was often threatened and even a month before his death was aware of the plot to kill him by prominent politicians. Although upset about the plot, he carried on as normal duties until his assassination.'

'Pio was murdered to silence him and put an end to his dream to implement socialism, the ideals for which the people of Kenya had formed a government. Now that Independence had been gained, and the armed forces' loyalty had been bought [British soldiers were still in Kenya to provide further security], those in power considered it a convenient time to assassinate Pinto as a warning to other dedicated nationalists,' he wrote in the tribute titled Pinto, My Brother.

We were greatly inspired by Pinto. We had to teach upcoming generations about him. At Mathare Social Justice Centre Matigari kids book club we had a class on his grave site at City Park cemetery Nairobi. We sang *Wimbo wa Mapambano* together and readout aloud the words engraved on his grave: If I have been extinguished, yet there arise a thousand beacons from the spark I bore.

Pio Gama Pinto, Ni Njamba wa Bururi.

REFLECTION 14: LEWIS MAGHANGA

The ever increasing political and economic strife, the ever widening gap between the rich and the poor, the increased militarism of global imperial forces, and the advent of neoliberalism all point to one thing; the class struggle, naturally, keeps getting more and more acute. As the society keeps getting more and more unequal, so does the need for the ruling classes to protect themselves more and more from the people, and, therefore, so does their thirst to maintain the monopoly of violence in a bid to keep the people enslaved.

What, therefore, does this mean for us? What are we to do?

The need for we as the people to resist this onslaught, as has been done for years and years, cannot be more imperative. For we, as the toiling people, this means nothing but desperate struggle to counter what we can comfortably call desperate resistance from the ruling elite. We have the responsibility to carry through the class struggle to its logical conclusion.

The essence of these reflections on *Pio Gama Pinto: Kenya's Unsung Martyr* is to vividly expose and highlight the ongoing class struggle that has been characteristic of the historical development of Kenya.

The bulk of the activity that Pio Gama Pinto engaged in, as clearly highlighted and explained in the book, was geared towards furthering this struggle, and was anchored upon his understanding of the laws of the development of the society.

Reflections

By the time Pio returned to Kenya from India in 1949, the anti-colonial fight had intensified with land and economic rights at the top of the agenda. Together with other organisers within the trade union and working class movement such as Makhan Singh, Fred Kubai and Bildad Kaggia, who had already laid the groundwork and established links between workers and peasants with radical politics, Pinto embarked on a militant approach in the anti-colonial struggle. Their strategy, as opposed to the moderate strategy of peacefully petitioning the colonial authorities for 'rights', correctly read the mood of the vast majority of the people of Kenya who were suffering greatly under the yoke of colonial exploitation. They organised strikes, which proved much more effective in helping the workers meet their demands.

It had become increasingly obvious that 'constitutional', 'non-violent' methods of fighting for one's rights was absolutely futile in dealing with the settler-colonial combination which was charged with the administration of the country. Organised violence was the only answer to such a situation.

In addition to helping the workers champion for better working conditions, the militant approach championed by Pinto and his allies helped improve the image of the working class movement among the masses, and boosted the confidence of the masses on the movement. It is this confidence in the power of the people that led to establishment of the Kenya Land and Freedom Army, popularly known as Mau Mau, to spearhead the struggle for Kenya's independence. The KLFA was the first armed liberation movement in Africa.

Pinto's involvement with the Mau Mau armed liberation struggle indicated his readiness to do whatever it took to realise the aspirations of the people of Kenya and to champion the cause of the working class throughout the world. Indeed, he recognised the need to support and take part in the proletarian struggle that engulfed the world and that had manifested itself in the struggle for self-determination of the people.

The run up to formal independence in Kenya saw Pinto getting involved in the national political party at that time, the Kenya African National Union (KANU). Perceiving independence as an end to exploitation, land alienation and imperialist influence, Pinto, together with Bildad Kaggia and other leftists, was the principal organiser of the section of KANU which was more left wing than Kenyatta, and which stuck to the genuine demands of the African people in their activities within KANU.

What, though, are the genuine demands of the African people in Kenya? Said Pinto,

> The sacrifices of the hundreds of thousands of Kenya's freedom fighters must be honoured by the effective implementation of the policy – a democratic, African, socialist state in which the people have the right to be free from economic exploitation and the right to social equality. Kenya's Uhuru must not be transformed into freedom to exploit, or freedom be hungry and live in ignorance. Uhuru must be

Uhuru for the masses – Uhuru from exploitation, from ignorance, disease and poverty.'[1]

It goes for a fact that the people of Kenya are interested in improving their material conditions of existence. Kenyans want access to land as the primary factor of production. Kenyans want food. Kenyans want access to quality healthcare, education, and decent housing. Kenyans want access to the basic necessities as well as the luxuries. Kenyans want peace, freedom and dignity. Kenyans want Socialism, and Pinto understood.

Politically, Pinto's views were beyond many in his depth of political understanding and social consciousness. To him Socialism meant its true application. Pinto lived his Socialism. He lived by his principles, and died by his principles. He was quick to react to any injustice, and he spent long hours helping other people.[2]

Throughout his political career, Pinto kept his focus on three aspects of political work; the need for a clear vision and ideological clarity – which in his case was socialism; the need for an organisation which could ensure that the vision was implemented – setting up organisations such as the Kenya Freedom Party and working with the progressive KANU party are examples; and reliance on working people and party cadres to bring about social and political change – setting up the Lumumba Institute was one such example. Without revolutionary theory there can be no revolutionary movement.[3]

Pinto became an important person in the struggle not only because of his clear ideological grasp of the situation and his total commitment to the liberation struggle but also because he linked different aspects of the struggle and ensured that all worked together to strengthen the overall anti-imperialist struggle.

The involvement of Pio Gama Pinto in the struggles of the Kenya Land and Freedom Army, FRELIMO in Mozambique as well as Goa, Angola and Guinea Bissau point towards his internationalism that is characteristic of Socialism. Internationalism, far from being an abstract idea, is a recognition of the global character of the economy as it is, and a representation of the advancement of the forces of production. Internationalism is an appreciation of the fact that the workers have no country. It is our knowledge of the fact

---

1. Page 91
2. Page 90
3. From 'What is to be done?', Lenin (1903)

that the struggle is to ultimately free every human being from exploitation and slavery, and to achieve the total abolition of classes.

Pinto's aim was a unified approach across Africa.[4] The unified front, akin to Ernesto Che Guevara's conception of a Common Front for all African Revolutionary Movements, would lead the people of Africa in combatting imperialism, neocolonialism and their agents all across the African continent. This Common Front would, if brought to existence, unite the struggling masses of Africa through their revolutionary movements. By unifying the people, it is needless to mention that the unification of Africa under a Socialist government would be attained.

Clearly, Pinto's Socialist, anti-imperialist and internationalist stance was a serious threat to the agents of capitalism and global imperialism. It is necessary to see the wider political reasons behind the assassination of Pinto as well as the immediate cause and events that led to his assassination. In essence, Pinto was the victim of the regressive, conservative forces, backed by imperialism, who came to power at independence. They immediately set about consolidating their position and eliminating all forces that did or could threaten their rule. The ground had been well prepared for them by the departing colonial power which ensured that Jomo Kenyatta, their favourite to maintain Kenya within the imperialist orbit, got maximum power and support.[5]

How, therefore, do we remember and acknowledge the contribution of Pio Gama Pinto to the struggles of the people of Kenya, Africa and the world?

The way to do this would be to carry through the International Proletarian Revolution. Our task is to pick up the rifle and keep fighting. We have to keep up the struggle as begun and continued by the pioneer revolutionaries of Africa. We have to create the Common Front, as envisioned by Pinto. We have to unite the people of Africa, and the way to do this is to unite our revolutionary movements. We must struggle together. We must unite all proletarian revolutionary parties into one giant organization. With this, we shall be able to carry through the tasks of our generation.

---

4. Page 78
5. Page 122

ABOUT THE CONTRIBUTORS

REFLECTION 1: Easther Waiguma Njoki, is a criminology and security studies graduate from Muranga University and community researcher, a member of Ghetto Foundation, and the Social Justice Movement.

REFLECTIONS 2: Lena Anyuolo is a writer and social justice activist. They are a member of Ukombozi Library and a member of the Organic Intellectual Network of the social justice movement in Kenya. As a writer – activist their work has appeared in Review of African Political Economy, Awaaz Magazine, Kenya Socialist, and Ukombozi Review. She is a co-editor and contributor in the series, 'Capitalism in my City' published on Africa is a Country.

REFLECTIONS 3: Gacheke Gachihi is the Coordinator of Mathare Social Justice Centre and member of Social Justice Centre Steering Committee.

REFLECTIONS 4: Kinuthia Ndung'u is a Community Volunteer and member of the Communist Party of Kenya.

REFLECTIONS 5: Minoo Kyaa is a member of Mukuru Community Justice Centre and the coordinator of Reggae for Social Justice. She is also a member of the Women in Social Justice Centres movement. She is a writer and a poet. Her art documents struggle and resistance.

REFLECTIONS 6: Lee-Anne Kaari Ndegwa is a student, videographer and member of the organic intellectual network.

REFLECTIONS 7: Gathanga Ndung'u is a biotechnologist and a community organizer with Ruaraka Social Justice Centre and part of Organic Intellectuals. He's a pan-africanist and socialist. He's passionate about African history, food security & sovereignty and ecological justice.

REFLECTIONS 8: Ezra Otieno is member of the Revolutionary Socialist League Central Committee.

REFLECTION 9: Davis Tafari is a social justice activist, member of Dandora Community Justice Centre and organic intellectual network

REFLECTIONS 10: Nicholas Mwangi is a Historian, Member of Ukombozi Library, Editor at the Organic intellectual network and co-founder of Dagoretti Social Justice Centre.

REFLECTIONS 11: Brian Mathenge is a Member of Githurai Social Justice, Justice Centers Working Group and Member of Communist Party of Kenya.

REFLECTIONS 12: Antony Adoyo is a member of the Dandora Community Justice Centre and Convener of the Participatory Action Research Committee of the Social Justice Centre Working Group (SJCWG) in Kenya.

REFLECTIONS 13: Mzalendo Wanjira Wanjiru is co-founder of Mathare Social Justice Center and a member of the social justice movement and founder of Matigari book club.

REFLECTIONS 14: Lewis Maghanga Njuguna is a writer and Political organiser and a member of the Organic Intellectuals Network. He holds a Bachelor's degree in Economics from the University of Nairobi.